MY FIRST LOOK AT HOLIDAYS

THE TORAH IS AN IMPORTANT BOOK FOR JEWS

Hanukkah

VALERIE BODDEN

CREATIVE EDUCATION

Published by Creative Education

123 South Broad Street, Mankato, Minnesota 56001

Creative Education is an imprint of The Creative Company

Designed by Rita Marshall

Photographs by Archive Photos, Bob Ecker, Beryl Goldberg, Terrance Klassen, Richard

Nowitz, Photri/Stock Imagery, P.C. Robinson

Cover illustration © 1996 Roberto Innocenti

Copyright © 2006 Creative Education

Printed in the United States of America

Library of Congress Cataloging-in-Publication Data

Bodden, Valerie. Hanukkah / by Valerie Bodden.

p. cm. — (My first look at holidays)

ISBN 1-58341-369-3

1. Hanukkah—Juvenile literature.

BM695.H3.B725 2005   296.4'35—dc22   2004056159

First edition 9 8 7 6 5 4 3 2 1

Hanukkah

THE HANUKKAH STORY

Hanukkah is a **holiday** celebrated by **Jews**. It is one of the world's oldest holidays. Hanukkah comes in November or December every year. It lasts for eight days.

Long ago, a king told the Jews they could not pray to God. So the Jews went to war against the king. They won, but their **temple** was destroyed.

A MENORAH IS A SPECIAL PART OF HANUKKAH

After the Jews cleaned and fixed the temple, they lit a special oil lamp. But they had only enough oil for one night. Then a **miracle** happened. The oil burned for eight nights. People celebrate this miracle on Hanukkah.

LIGHTING CANDLES

Some people call Hanukkah the "**Festival** of Lights." Jews light a menorah on Hanukkah. A menorah is a special candleholder. It holds nine candles.

Shalom means "peace."
People use it to say
hello and good-bye in
some Jewish countries.

THIS JEWISH TEMPLE IS IN A CITY CALLED JERUSALEM

MENORAHS COME IN MANY DIFFERENT SHAPES

Eight of the candles are for the eight days of Hanukkah. The ninth candle is a helper candle. It is used to light the other candles. It stands in the middle of the menorah.

On the first night of Hanukkah, Jews light one candle. On the second night, they light two candles. They add a candle every night until all eight are lit.

Long ago, menorahs
were not lit with candles.
They were lit with olive oil.

People pray when they light the candles. Sometimes they sing songs, too. They let the candles burn for at least 30 minutes.

Special Foods

Jews eat special foods during Hanukkah. They cook many of these foods in oil. This is to remember the oil that burned for eight days in the temple.

PEOPLE LIGHT CANDLES FOR THE "FESTIVAL OF LIGHTS"

One special food is called a latke. Latkes are pancakes made from potatoes. They are fried in oil. They are crispy on the outside and soft on the inside. Some people eat latkes with applesauce. Others eat them with sour cream.

Many people eat cheese and cheesecake during Hanukkah. Others eat special jelly-filled donuts. Some people eat fried balls of dough with honey.

One special kind of
Hanukkah cake is made
from 44 different ingredients.

POTATO PANCAKES CALLED LATKES

Presents and Games

Jewish kids usually get small presents for each day of Hanukkah. Gelt is a popular present. The word "gelt" means "money." Hanukkah gelt is usually made of chocolate. But sometimes it can be real money, too.

WOODEN DREIDELS AND A HANDFUL OF GELT

A dreidel is another popular present. A dreidel has four sides and spins like a top. Kids play a game called "Spin the Dreidel" with it. During Hanukkah, people like to play chess and card games, too.

Hanukkah is a special holiday for Jewish people. It is a time families get together, pray, and have fun!

The letters on the

sides of a dreidel mean

"A great miracle happened there."

SOME JEWS READ FROM THE TORAH AT HANUKKAH

Hands-on: Marshmallow Menorah

Make a Hanukkah menorah with marshmallows!

What You Need

A piece of cardboard about
   the size of a ruler
10 large colored marshmallows

Frosting
A plastic knife
Nine birthday candles

What You Do

1. Spread frosting on the bottom of nine marshmallows. Put them in a straight line, frosting-side down, on the cardboard.
2. Spread frosting on top of the middle marshmallow. Put another marshmallow on top of it.
3. Stick a candle in each marshmallow.
4. Have a grown-up help you light your menorah. Light one candle each day until all eight are lit!

A Jewish boy reading stories about God

Index

Words to Know

festival—a celebration with a lot of food and fun

holiday—a special day that happens every year

Jews—people who believe in God, part of the Bible, and a book called the Talmud

miracle—when something happens that seems impossible

temple—a place for Jews to pray to God

Read More

Johnston, M. C. *Hanukkah*. Chanhassen, Minn.: The Child's World, 2003.

Kimmelman, Leslie. *Hanukkah Lights, Hanukkah Nights*. New York: HarperCollins Publishers, 1992.

Rosinsky, Natalie M. *Hanukkah*. Minneapolis, Minn.: Compass Point Books, 2003.

Explore the Web

Billy Bear's Hanukkah http://www.billybear4kids.com/holidays/hanukkah/hanukkah.htm

Lil' Fingers: Happy Hanukkah http://www.lil-fingers.com/holidays/hanukkah/index.html

Torah Tots http://www.torahtots.com/holidays/chanuka/chanuk.htm